The

By
W. BEN HUNT

and

JOHN J. METZ

PO Box 233
Azle, TX 76098

Copyright, 1936–1939
W. Ben Hunt
Printed in Canada
(Eighth Printing — 1944)

CONTENTS

Introduction 3

The Flat Bow 5

The Bowstring 22

Arrows 27

Tackle 41

Shooting 48

Short Cuts 58

Flat Bows from Square Staves 65

INTRODUCTION

Many look upon archery, once the sport of kings, as a pastime to be indulged in only by the well-to-do. This booklet, however, shows how even a boy equipped with little more than a knife, a saw, and a file or two, can make usable and efficient archery equipment.

Not satisfied with this, however, the book shows how the worker equipped with proper hand or power tools can make bows, arrows, and archery tackle which will stand favorable comparison with the archery equipment found anywhere.

This book confines itself to the making of the American bow — the flat bow. This is done, first, because there are many books available describing how the English long bow is made, and, second, because the flat bow, while it is as efficient as the English bow, requires less material and can be more easily made than the latter.

The authors gratefully acknowledge the assistance received from many sources. Especially do they wish to thank Larry Whiffen, Walter Fahsel, Warren Voth, W. C. Rohde, Bruce Robertson, and Clifford Dory, all members of the Milwaukee Archery Group, for many useful and practical hints that will assist the boy or man who wishes to make his own bows, arrows, and tackle.

Their thanks also are extended to Howard Hill, Los Angeles, Calif., for a number of beautiful pictures, and to Major Charles L. Williams, Champlain Valley Archers, Keeseville, N. Y., for some very helpful criticisms, most of which were embodied in the revised edition.

The authors also hope that their little book will be an aid in furthering the revival of that famous sport of Robin Hood — archery.

The Flat Bow

If you have never watched an archery meet or tournament, you should do so before attempting to make archery equipment. To stand back of the shooting line and watch the action of the different styles of bows is extremely worth while. One archer seemingly will aim to shoot away over the target, but his arrow falls short of it, while next to him will be one who uses an almost point-blank aim. You will see English bows, flat bows, recurved bows, bows backed with fiber, bows backed with rawhide, and some without any backing, and you will wonder which is the best one of the lot. Yet, each archer likes his particular bow because he is accustomed to it.

There is much information available on the making

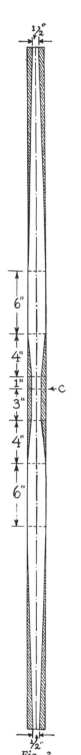

Fig. 3

Fig. 1

of the English long bow. For that reason the description in this book will be confined to the different kinds of flat bows. These bows might be called American bows, as the Indians made and used them, but no Indian ever made as nice a shooting bow as the modern flat bow. The Indian bows usually are rather crude affairs, which bend as much at the handle as at the ends. They were used as hunting bows and were not designed for target shooting at 100 yards.

The Flat Bow

When making a bow, it is well to make it of real bow wood. Yew and osage orange are probably a little beyond the range of the average pocketbook. Good lemonwood is excellent, while locust and rock elm are good woods for bows intended for small boys.

Hickory makes very serviceable bows, especially when they are recurved. Get white or second-growth hickory. The darker heartwood is rather brittle. No matter which wood is used, if the directions are followed closely, the archer will get a good bow. In all bow woods except lemonwood, the grain should run as shown in Figure 1, the top being the back of the bow. With lemonwood, grain doesn't matter, and it is for that reason that it is easiest to work. However, lemonwood has cross grain like all wood has. At times it can be detected only in working as the grain of the wood does not show.

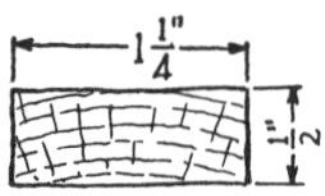

The usual lemonwood staves are 1 by 1 in. or 1⅛ by 1⅛ in. by 6 ft. Directions for making a bow from such a stave are given in the last chapter of this book.

The best stave for a flat bow is about 1¼ to 1½ in. wide by ½ to ⅝ in. thick and 6 ft. long. Plane the side intended for the back of the bow and sight along it to see if it is straight. Bow woods are frequently warped. If the stave is warped, draw the

Fig. 2

[6]

center line down the center of it as in Figure 3. If the ends are checked or split, cut them off. A bow of this type may vary in length from 5 ft. to 6 ft.

Next, lay off the center of the stave and mark it. This center is shown at C in Figure 3. Then measure off 1 in. one way and 3 in. the other way from the center. This is for the grip or handle. Then measure 4 in. each way from these two lines and again 6 in. each way from the last two lines. Figures 3 and 4, show clearly how these cross lines are laid out on the stave. Then at the ends, mark off ¼ in. on each side of the center line. This makes the nock ends ½ in. wide in the rough. Next, mark off the width of the grip as shown. The grip should be at least 1 in. wide and some times wider for a man's hand or on a strong bow.

Draw two parallel lines the length of the grip and connect the ends of these two lines to the ends of the lines marked A in Figure 4. From the lines marked B, Figure 4, draw lines to points located ¼ in. from the center line at each end.

Figure 3 shows how the bow should look at this time. In laying out a warped stave, be sure that the widths from the center line to the outer edges at A and B, as shown in Figure 4, are equal.

Next, cut away the surplus wood with a spokeshave or a band saw and round off at A and B to form a slight curve.

The block for the handle may be glued on before or after cutting away the surplus wood. The block may be of walnut, mahogany, or gumwood, and should be as wide as the widest part of the bow, ⅞ to 1 in. thick and from 12 to 14 in. long as shown in Figure 5. Use casein glue for this job, applied as directed on page 16. Shape the handle as shown in Figure 6.

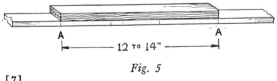

Fig. 5

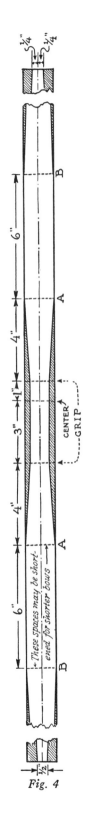

Fig. 4

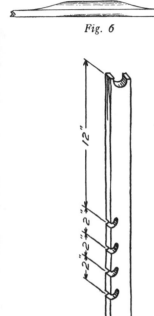

Fig. 6

Fig. 7

The final shaping of the bow now begins, but before it is started, a rig for tillering the bow must be made. *Tillering* means bending the bow while in the process of making, to determine whether or not it is bending properly. The simplest method is with a tillering stick fashioned from a piece of wood ⅞ by 2 by 24 in. shaped as shown in Figure 7. In tillering, the center of the handle of the bow must be placed into the hollowed end of the stick shown in Figure 7, and the string pulled into the notches. See Figure 8.

Chalk lines are drawn on the floor as indicated in Figure 8, and when the tillered bow is laid down as shown, the irregularities of the bow are readily seen.

Another and better way is to fasten the tillering jig, shown in Figure 9, to the wall.

This jig is better than the tillering stick if more bows are to be made. It takes but a minute to lay the bow on the support, hook on the string and pull — a little way at first, and as far as one wishes after the bow gets worked down more. Lines are drawn on the wall for gauging the curve.

The bow must be trimmed down carefully with a sharp spokeshave until the sections shown in Figure 10 have been obtained. The back should have a slight arc, while the belly is rounded more. Now file the nocks as shown in Figure 11. This is done with a small rat-tail file, first rounding off the ends of the bow. Do

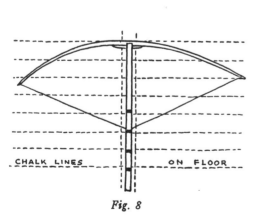

Fig. 8

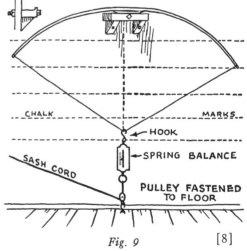

Fig. 9

not run the nock around the back, as this weakens the bow at that point. A piece of fiber or horn glued to the back of the tip where the nocks are cut, as shown in Figure 11A, will do much to strengthen the ends of the bow. Next, get a strong piece of cord about ⅛ in. thick (no thicker) and loop the ends over the nocks so as to have about 3 or 4 in. clearance at the grip. The proper bracing of the bow will be taken up later. Put the bow on the tillering stick or jig, whichever has been made, and pull to 12 in. This will give a first idea of how strong the bow is.

Before going any further, it may be well to say a few words about the pull of a bow. For the average boy, a pull of from 14 to 20 pounds at the full draw (to the cheek) is ample. A girl's or woman's bow should have a pull of from 14 to 35 lbs. For a man it should be 30 to 50 pounds. A spring fish scale hooked on the wall tillering jig will give you this poundage. Too strong a bow is hard to handle and takes the joy out of archery. After the muscles become accustomed to this form of exercise, one can always make a stronger bow. But it is well to start out with a light bow. It will be easier on the fingers, too.

If the bow is too strong, scrape off a little at a time from the belly side until the pull has been reduced the required amount. The bow should have an even bend starting at about 6 in. from each side of the center. If the bow bends only at the ends, it is said to be whip ended, and if it bends too much in the middle, the bow will kick or jar. See Figure 12. If one end bends more than the other, shave off a little from the stiffer limb.

GRIP

WIDEST PART "A"

⅓ FROM END "B"

1½" FROM END

Fig. 10

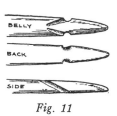

Fig. 11

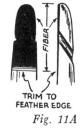

Fig. 11A

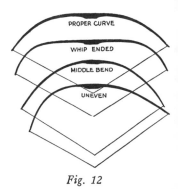

Fig. 12

Fig. 13

For scraping, use glass, a cabinet scraper, or a piece of an old power hack-saw blade about 1 in. wide, from which the teeth have been ground off. These hack-saw scrapers cannot be filed. Be careful not to take off too much at a time while scraping, and put the bow on the tiller frequently until the proper curve has been secured. This procedure requires patience. Try pulling the bow as in shooting to see how it feels and how it fits the hand. Don't try to see how far it can be pulled at first. Take the cord off the bow for a day or two, then tiller the bow again to see if one side or the other has let down. If one limb pulls to one side, scrape off the convex side to bring it back into line. Weakening one part makes another part proportionately stronger. The only way to strengthen a bow that has become too weak is by shortening it. But this sometimes also shortens the pull. A bow $5\frac{1}{2}$ to 6 ft. long will take a 28-in. arrow. Shorter bows will require proportionately shorter arrows. An average man pulls a 26 to 28-in. arrow to the pile or ferrule.

After the bow seems to have the correct pull and weight, take it out and shoot with it for a while before finishing it. The grip, however, should first be wrapped with braided fishline, or leather or plush may be glued on. To wrap it, use trolling line, and after the grip is nicely wrapped and the cord ends are concealed, soak it well with shellac or lacquer and set it away to dry. Figure 13 shows how a neatly wrapped grip should look. As said before, use the bow for a while and watch for any weakening. If one limb shows weakening, shave a little more off the other one.

The line up

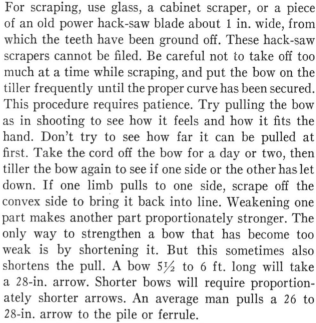

Fig. 14

When the bow has demonstrated its fitness, sand it down carefully and apply a coat of shellac. When dry, rub it down with 2/0 steel wool and give it a coat of spar varnish or clear lacquer. Rub it down again very lightly with 2/0 steel wool.

It will be noticed that the bow will follow the string somewhat, that is, it will take a slight curve after the bow is unstrung. This is not disturbing, however, as this slight set will not increase. One should never try to overcome it by bending the bow in the opposite direction.

To string or brace a bow properly, the bowstring should be a fistmele from the bow, as shown in Figure 14.

Keep the bow where it will not dry out and also where it is not too moist. Always hang it on a wooden peg, as shown in Figure 15. Do not hang it on a nail, as that might cause a rust spot.

For directions for making flat bows from square staves, see page 65.

Fig. 15

The Recurved Bow

It seems everyone admires a recurved bow. There is something fascinating about this type of bow, which is shown in Figure 16. The old English long bows were frequently equipped with horn tips designed to give the bow the appearance of a recurved bow. Besides beauty of line, the recurved bow usually has a better cast. This type of bow makes a fine hunting bow, though it is not essentially a target bow.

To make a recurved bow like the one shown in Figures 16 and 18, requires steaming. Some bow woods

Figs. 16, 17, and 18

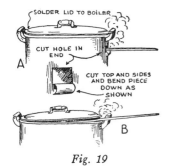

Fig. 19

can be steamed and bent more readily than others. Oregon yew, Osage orange, and hickory are best for recurving, while with lemonwood only a slight curve can be put into the ends. If, then, the bowyer is fortunate enough to have a stave of yew, Osage orange, or hickory, the steaming will be easy. With lemonwood he will have to steam the ends longer in order to get them soft enough for bending. If a number of bows are to be steamed, it is advisable to make a steaming tank of a washboiler as shown at A in Figure 19. If only one or two bows are to be recurved, a wash boiler may be used as shown at B in Figure 19. Stick the bow ends into the boiler at one end, fit the cover in at the other end, and let it rest on the bow or bows, as shown in Figure 19 at B. Then throw on old gunny sack or piece of soft carpet over the cover and tuck it around the part of the bow which projects. Do not, however, tuck it in too tightly, or mother may need a new boiler and her boy may need a hospital bed.

A bow that is recurved but slightly may be made by gluing a block of hardwood such as beefwood, black walnut, any of the bow woods, or a piece of fiber at each end of the stave as shown at A in Figure 20. The ends must then be shaped as shown at B in Figure 20.

The string grooves in the ends of a recurved bow must extend as far from the nock as the string touches the bow. This means also that the end should be a little thicker to compensate for the wood taken out

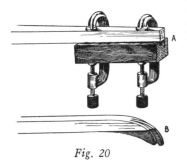

Fig. 20

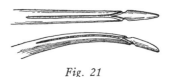

Fig. 21

[12]

for these grooves. Figure 21 shows how these grooves are to be cut, but this must not be done until after the ends are steamed. Figure 22 shows another way in which these grooves and nocks may be cut, but this calls for a bit of careful whittling.

Another thing to remember when making a recurved bow is that the handle is not to be glued on until after the ends have been steamed. It is well also to leave enough wood on the ends to allow for some cutting down. Before beginning the steaming, the bending form shown in Figure 23 must be made. A piece of 2-in. plank will be required for this. After cutting the end of the plank to the radius shown, fasten a loop of band iron, as shown at A in Figure 23, to the plank with a couple of stove bolts. This loop should have enough opening to hold the end of the bow.

To prevent the bow end from splitting while it is being bent, place a piece of strap iron 1 or 1½ in. wide by 1/16 in. thick and 12 in. long over it as shown in Figure 24. For lemonwood, the loop should be placed as at B, in Figure 23, and the lemonwood should be steamed for at least an hour. Next put about 2 in. of water in the boiler, and put one end of the bow in. Yew, Osage, locust, or hickory require from 30 to 45 minutes of actual steaming.

Get the form ready and have the clamp properly set. If clamps are not available, use rope to tie the bow to the form. After the end has been properly steamed, put it into the loop, place the piece of iron over it, and with an even pressure bend it to the form as

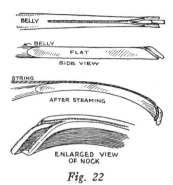

Fig. 22

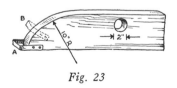

Fig. 23

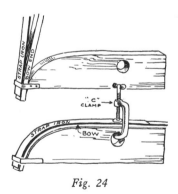

Fig. 24

shown in Figure 24. The bending should be done smoothly, without haste, but there is no time to waste or the wood will cool off and the steaming will have to be done all over again — or probably it will be necessary to make a new bow.

If rope is used, wrap it around the whole plank.

Allow the bow to remain on the form for four hours or longer. Steam and bend the other end in the same way. Then glue the handle in place. The bow should then be hung up somewhere to dry for about a week to be sure all the moisture is out of the ends.

The bow is then ready for the nocks which should be carefully cut or filed with a rat-tail file and the rest of the end worked down to shape. Then file the string groove and the bow is ready for tillering and working down to a proper curve. It is a bit harder to string a recurved bow than a straight bow, but with a little practice the knack will be acquired. The beginner should be careful not to get his fingers under the string.

Next, sight the bow as shown in Figure 25, to see if the bending has been properly done. If not, the bow may have to be steamed over again.

It may be noticed that after the bow has dried, the curve has probably straightened out a bit, but just as with *following the string,* there will be only a definite amount of flattening out, after which the curve will remain the same.

After the tillering and scraping have been done, the bow is ready for finishing. Lemonwood takes

Fig. 25

walnut stain very nicely. This wood also may show up small flaws at this stage of the work. These appear in the form of checks as shown in Figure 26. Should these checks show up at the curves, it would be well to wrap the bow at this point with fine hemp or heavy silk set in glue, as shown in Figure 27. Buttonhole silk answers the purpose very well for this. Wrapping a bow does not harm its looks, in fact it sometimes adds to its appearance, and it has saved many a bow from breaking.

For directions for making a setback bow, see page 67.

Backed Bows

Bows may be backed in a number of ways. Sometimes a bow is backed with a thin piece of hickory which is the toughest of all bow woods, but usually the backings are fiber or rawhide. Fiber is the easiest to obtain and to apply, and rawhide, while probably the best, is also the trickiest to apply. The backing is used mainly to keep the bow from breaking. It does not, however, add much cast to the bow.

A hickory-backed walnut bow, which has been in use for over two years, is still in good condition. One large recurved walnut bow with fiber backing shot a flight arrow 341 yards.

For a hickory-backed walnut bow, choose walnut that is straight-grained, and the hickory should be straight-grained whitewood or sapwood. The back of the bow, where the two woods are to be glued together, must be planed perfectly flat, with a hand or a power jointer.

Fig. 26

Fig. 27

The pattern or lines of the bow should be of the flat-bow type described in this article. The piece of walnut should be about 6 ft. long by 1½ by ⅜ in. and planed as true as possible. The piece of hickory should be of the same length and width but only 3/16 in. thick.

Casein glue is the most reliable glue for any work on archery equipment. Mix this glue strictly according to the directions given by the manufacturer. If the glue is too thin or too thick it will not function properly.

Before beginning the gluing operation, get the clamps ready. A piece of 1 by 2-in. pine, 6 ft. long, also will be required. If iron C clamps are being used, have some small thin pieces of wood or cardboard ready to put under the jaws to prevent disfiguring the bow stave. The iron vise may be used as an additional clamp.

Put a thin layer of glue on each jointed face and let it set for 20 minutes. To eliminate all lumps, smooth the glue with the fingers.

Next spread a thick second layer of glue over each piece and then place the two together. Put the piece of 2-in. pine back of the hickory and put the whole in the vise, as shown in Figure 28.

Then place the other clamps at regular intervals along on both sides of the vise. As many as 16 clamps plus the vise may be used on a 6-ft. bow. Be careful that the pieces of wood do not slip sidewise while applying the pressure.

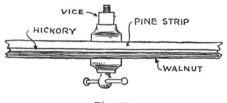

Fig. 28

If the worker has no clamps, he may wrap the three pieces of wood with a good piece of washline. To do this, after placing the two glued pieces together, let them remain a few minutes under some slight pressure, and after placing the pine strip next to the hickory, tie the ends with a piece of heavy cord or rope. Then proceed to wrap the three pieces of wood spirally as tight as possible with the rope. Then drive small wedges under the rope at intervals to further increase the pressure. Figure 29 shows a section of such a wrapped bow. Notice that the pressure is great enough to cause the glue to ooze out on both sides. Allow the glue to dry for at least 24 hours; 48 would be better. Do not try to bend the bow for a week at least. The stave can be worked into shape without being bent. When the clamps or ropes are off, scrape off the glue on the edges and then proceed as with the flat bow. Round off the belly or walnut part of the bow a little more than the back which should have only a slight curve. See Figure 30.

Fig. 29

The handle is glued on as on any flat bow. It may be made of walnut or of a light colored wood for contrast. It also may be wrapped with a light trolling line if so desired. Then the bow must be tillered until the correct curve is attained.

The man who wants to back his bow with fiber has four colors of fiber to choose from: red, black, gray, and white. There doesn't seem to be any difference between these colored fibers as far as strength is concerned.

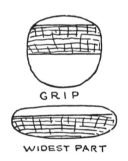

GRIP

WIDEST PART

NARROW SECTION

Fig. 30

Fiber can be bought at electrical supply houses, and in some cities there are dealers who sell fiber only. It should be at least 1/16 in. thick, but no thicker than 3/32 in. It would be better if it could be obtained in 5½ to 6-ft. lengths, but it usually comes in 3-ft. sheets from which the strips are cut. They must then be butted together in the center of the grip or handle, and a piece of the same wood used for the grip, about ⅛ in. thick, should be glued over the handle on the back. A fiber-backed bow is made the same as the backed bow already described, excepting that the back is not to be rounded at all.

Cut the strips of fiber a trifle narrower than the stave. The fiber must then be soaked in warm water for several hours. In the meantime, prepare the casein glue and then tear some light canvas, duck, or muslin into strips from 1 to 1½ in. wide. The longer these strips are, the better. By this time the fiber should be soft and pliable, but it should not be allowed to become too flexible.

Wipe the surplus water off the fiber, and coat one side with glue. Give the wood a coat of glue also, and let both lie for a few minutes until the glue is tacky, but not dry. Then apply a good second coat of glue over the fiber and lay it on the wood. Whether the fiber is in one long piece or in two short pieces, the wrapping should start at the handle, and go both ways. *Stretch the fiber* by pulling with the hands only, and wrap it carefully to the ends. With the aid of an assistant this wrapping job may be easily done. In the

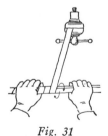

Fig. 31

absence of a helper, fasten one end of the cloth in a vise and roll the bow along it, as shown in Figure 31, being careful to keep the fiber centered on the wood. The cloth should overlap as you go along. See Figure 32. Don't be afraid of getting glue on the hands, as this is a rather messy job. Wrap right up to the ends and tie with a piece of string. When you are through with the wrapping, let the glue dry thoroughly before the wrapping is taken off. This may take several days. The bow is then formed like any other bow, and if the glue job has been well done, one need have no fear of the fiber loosening up while working on the bow. Shape it as shown in Figure 33, and glue a thin piece of wood about 4 in. long over the fiber at the handle to round it off nicer. Fiber takes a beautiful finish after it has been sanded down, but as some kinds have rather rough surfaces, it takes quite a bit of sanding to get it smooth.

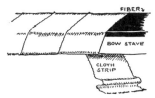

Fig. 32

While casein glue is waterproof, it is always good policy to varnish backed bows and keep them away from excessive heat, cold, and dampness.

While on the subject of backed bows, a word might be said about rawhide backing. Several archery-supply houses sell backed staves on which the rawhide has the thickness of heavy wrapping paper. Rawhide can be obtained, however, which is $\frac{1}{8}$ in. thick. With such a substantial backing, a beautiful bow may be made, but to make it requires much work and experience. Furthermore, these bows are not to be looked upon as indestructible. They must be handled with care at

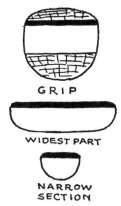

Fig. 33

[19]

all times, and should not be drawn further than the draw they were made for. This means that if a bow has been used for shooting 28-in. arrows, it should not be tried out to see how far it will shoot one that is 30 in. long. It might shoot farther, and then again it might just snap in two, and probably give the incautious archer a good crack across the head.

Care of the Bow

Some archers use an oiled rag for wiping their bows before putting them away. Others use regular furniture wax. The latter method is preferable because it gives the bow a more lasting coating.

Arrows should be treated in the same manner.

Do not throw a bow down on the ground or on the grass. If dampness doesn't harm it, someone may step on it. Set it up against a tree or shrub where it is out of the way. When carrying a bow on the train, in a street car, or in an auto, it is good policy to have a bow case.

At home, the bows should be hung up where the temperature remains fairly uniform. Some archers build a rack for their bows.

Do not let anyone try your bow to see how it pulls unless with an arrow in place, and let it be your own arrow. He may be using a longer arrow.

Playfully snapping the taut string of a bow is just as bad as snapping the trigger on an unloaded gun.

*Youthful archers at a boys' camp, Eagle River, Wis.
Larry Whiffen, Instructor*

When a bow has assumed a curve, that is, when it follows the string when unstrung, do not try to bend it backwards. If it is a good bow, it will not alter its shape after it has once assumed a certain set.

Don't keep a bow strung when not in use.

Extreme heat or cold do not help the bow in any way. In very cold weather, it is apt to break, and in very warm weather, it loses cast. When using a bow in cold weather, allow it to become thoroughly chilled before using.

Waiting their turn

Howard Hill with mule deer which he killed with a broadhead arrow

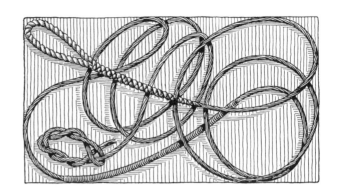

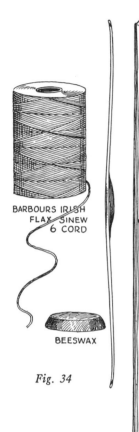

Fig. 34

The Bowstring

The bowstring plays an important part in archery. It must withstand strenuous usage and as it is continually pulled and jerked violently, it must be made of material which does not stretch. Irish flax or linen has been found to answer well for this purpose. Barbour's Irish flax sinew (6-cord) is the easiest to obtain and can be bought wherever shoemakers' supplies are sold. As it is obtainable only in a large ball, which at the present time costs about two dollars, and as there are many bowstrings in a ball, it is best for several to club together to buy it. Besides this, some thin flax, such as Barbour's No. 12 or some heavy silk thread or fine linen fishline, will be required for serving or wrapping. Beeswax also is one of the items needed.

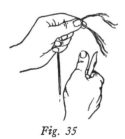

Fig. 35

How the String is Made

The bowstring described here is very easily and quickly made. Wally Gardoki, a Milwaukee archer and manufacturer of archery equipment, makes strings of the type described at the rate of twelve per hour.

The directions given are for a 6-strand string. A 9-strand bowstring can be made the same way except that the worker divides the strands into three groups of 3 strands each and then proceeds in the manner as with the two groups of strings.

1. Prepare 6 strands of No. 6 Barbour's flax sinew, each about 18 in. longer than the bow for which the bowstring is to be made. Since a string of this length is rather awkward to handle, keep the floor clean while making the bowstring, so that nothing will adhere to the waxed string.

Hold the strands in the left hand as shown in Figure 35, and divide them into two groups of 3 strands each. Then fray and at the same time taper the ends as shown.

2. Wax each of the two ends thus formed, for a length of 12 in., using the beeswax freely. See Figure 36.

Fig. 36

3. Still holding the string in the left hand as shown in Figure 37, twist evenly but not tightly, 8 or 8½ in. of the ends of each group. This is done to make all the strands lie parallel, and not over and across each other.

Fig. 37

4. Continue to hold the string with the left hand, and grasp one of the groups about 1 inch from the left finger tips. See Figure 38. Twist this tightly to

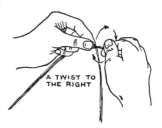

Fig. 38

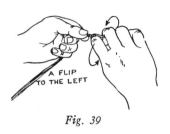

Fig. 39

the right between the right thumb and forefinger as shown. Then without loosening the grip, bring it toward you over the other group by a twist of the wrist, and sliding the thumb and forefingers of the left hand upward, hold it in place. See Figures 39 and 40.

5. Now do the same with the other group, twisting tightly to the right, flipping the twisted part over the first one and toward you, and again hold it with the thumb and forefingers of the left hand to keep it from untwisting.

Continue this process until enough has been twisted (3 to 3½ in.), to form the loop or eye.

6. Now form the loop (Fig. 41) laying the two ends along the two groups of long strands, which will form the body of the string.

7. Figure 42 shows one group of strands twisted together slightly, and the other one being straightened out. At A in Figure 43 is shown how the loop or eye looks when it is ready for the splice.

8. Hold the eye in the left hand, with the thumb and finger tips just covering the intersection at X in Figure 43. Now take a short hold again as shown in Figure 38 and twist and flip as when twisting the eye. See Figures 38, 39, and 40.

Twist to right and flip over loose strand to the left, always holding the last twist with the thumb and fingers of the left hand to keep it from untwisting. Continue this to the end of the tapered strands and the splice is finished.

Sometimes the beginner does not follow instructions

Fig. 40

Fig. 41

explicitly, usually neglecting to taper the ends properly. This produces a poor job which can be remedied, however, by serving the string at that point. If each strand is carefully tapered and frayed, however, the ends will taper down smoothly.

9. The eye or loop is now hooked over a nail or screw hook fastened high enough to reach easily, and the six strands are carefully waxed separately. They are laid straight by holding them at the ends and shifting them around. They should not lie over one another.

Now, while pulling to give them all an equal tension, tie a knot at the very end.

10. There are two methods of twisting the string proper. One is by twisting with the fingers, holding the string at the very end. This twist should be *toward the left,* as that is the direction of the last twisting of the splice.

Another method is to tie the end of the string to a piece of iron weighing about 5 lb. Then place the eye over a hook in the ceiling, or suspend it from a wall bracket and start the weight spinning toward the left. Keep this weight spinning until the bowstring is twisted sufficiently.

11. With the string still suspended from the hook, and with the other end tied to some object, or held by someone to keep it as taut as possible, wax it thoroughly over its entire length.

12. Then take a piece of soft leather or some brown wrapping paper and rub the entire string briskly. This warms and partially melts the wax and unites

Fig. 42

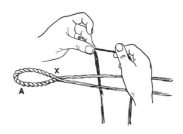

Fig. 43

[25]

Fig. 44

the strands into a real bowstring. If colored paper is used for rubbing, a pleasing tint may be given to the cord.

The usual fastening at the lower nock is with a timber hitch, tied as shown in Figure 44.

The string just described will take a bow of any weight up to 50 lb. If a heavier string is wanted, use 9 strands of the 6-cord Barbour's Irish flax sinew instead of 6 as for the string just described. To form the loop on this heavier string, make 3 groups instead of 2, and proceed just as with the lighter string.

After the bow has been properly braced, the string should be served at the nocking place to a thickness of almost $\frac{1}{8}$ in. and long enough to cover that portion of the string touched by the fingers while shooting. This saves the string from wear and at the same time is easier on the fingers. This serving should be done while the bow is braced. Sometimes the string is served with a contrasting color at the exact point of nocking to assist the archer when shooting.

Arrows

The most exacting part of making archery equipment is the production of the arrow. An Indian once said to Maurice Thompson (father of archery in this country as far as the white man is concerned), "Any stick do for bow, a good arrow — heap work." If the shaft is warped, or the pile is askew, or the feathers are put on wrong, an arrow will not function properly. Neither will an arrow with a shaft that is too thick, too heavy, too thin, or too weak. The standard diameter for a target arrow is 5/16 in., for a hunting arrow ⅜ in., while a flight arrow used only for distance, may be 5/16 in. at the thickest part, and 3/16 in. at the thinnest. Target arrows for ladies' bows are often made 9/32 in. in diameter.

All three of these styles of arrows will be described

Murry Yantis, Austin, Texas, setting a record of 439 yds. with a 65-lb. bow

in this article. While the easiest way of making arrows is to buy 5/16-in. dowels of birch or of Port Orford cedar, good arrows may be made without incurring much expense.

Inexpensive Arrows

Along country roads and in woods, one may find shoots of ash, hazel nut, willow, alder, or any other straight shoots that have no small branches. They should be about ½ in. thick at the butt and should not taper too much. Cut them about 30 in. long and peel off the bark before it dries. Then take a bunch of 15 or 20 and tie the butt ends together with some heavy cord as shown in Figure 49.

By bending and forcing a little here and there, they should be laid quite straight. Then starting at the butt end, wrap them together as tightly as possible, carrying the wrapping all the way up to the thin ends, and always watching that the shafts are laid straight. Tie the end of the bundle securely, as shown in Figure 50, and hang it up to dry with the butt ends down. If hung in a dry place, the shafts will be in condition in about a month or two, and will then be quite straight, although there may be slight irregularities.

Now take a 1-in. board about 30 in. long, and 2½ or 3 in. wide and cut a V out of one edge. See Figure 51. Regardless of the kind of arrows to be made, this will be found to be an exceedingly handy jig. Drive a nail or a screw about ½ in. from the end, as shown in Figure

Fig. 49

Fig. 50

Fig. 51

51 to act as a stop for the arrow to rest against while it is being worked upon.

Square up the shaft by cutting about ½ in. off the butt end, then cut them to a uniform length of 28 in. Place the V board in a vise and lay the shaft in the groove with the butt end against the nail, and dress it down with a small plane, turning the stick after every cut to keep it round. These arrows need not be of uniform diameter, that is, the butt may be slightly thicker than the nock or feathered end, but the shaft should be even and smooth and have an average diameter of about 5/16 in.

Fig. 52

The next step is to sand each stick carefully. The butt ends may then be wrapped for ½ in. with what is known as stovepipe wire, and a nail or screw driven in as shown in Figure 52. This will make a fairly good arrow point, or pile, as the archer would say.

The shaft is then ready for the nock. Clamp the shaft into the vise. For this purpose the vise jaws should be equipped with wood faces into which depressions have been filed so that the shaft may be held without being defaced with vise marks. See Figure 53.

Cut the nocks with three hack-saw blades fastened or tied together. This gives them the correct width. The depth of the nocks should be 3/16 in. to ¼ in. and the bottom should be rounded out with a rat-tail file. The end of the shaft should then be rounded off as shown in Figure 54 with a flat file or a piece of sandpaper.

Molded arrow nocks offer quite a short cut to the

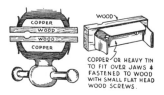

Fig. 53

Fig. 54

arrowmaker. These nocks are made of pyroxylin, and are obtainable in colors to match the arrow markings or milady's shooting costume. The nock end of the shaft is pointed with a pencil sharpener, some Dupont

Molded arrow nocks

cement is put on the point thus produced, and the nock is pressed in place.

The shafts are then ready for the feathers. Putting on the feathers is called fletching the arrow. For arrows to be used for roving or just shooting around where arrows are likely to be lost, almost any kind of large wing feathers will do. Very nice arrows have been made with pigeon, chicken, and duck feathers.

Cutting feathers for arrows troubles many archery enthusiasts, but it really requires patience, rather than skill.

Make a feather clamp by soldering two pieces of iron or brass to a large paper clamp as shown in Figure 55. Strip off the narrow vane of the feather by grasping it as shown in Figure 56 and pulling it off. Then with a shears, cut away ½ of the stem, cutting along the indentation on the hollow side of the stem as indicated in Figure 57. Another way of handling the job is to cut the feather into 2½-in. or 3-in sections. Then place one section into the clamp as shown

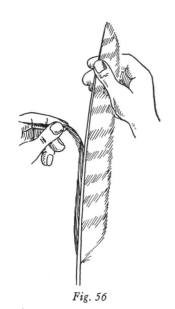

Fig. 56

Fig. 57

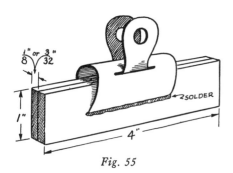

Fig. 55

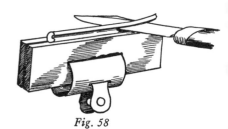

Fig. 58

in Figure 58, after which most of the stem may be cut off with a sharp knife.

Next tack a piece of coarse sandpaper, or better still, emery or carborundum cloth (coarse) to the top of a table or workbench, and holding the clamp as shown in Figure 59, at right angles to the abrasive cloth, grind down the rest of the stem, rubbing lengthwise, until only a very thin strip is left for holding the vane. If a sanding disk is available, the stems may be ground off on it. All that will be needed is a rest which permits holding the clamp at right angles to the disk. See Figure 115.

It will be noted that one side of the stem that is left will be thicker than the other. This is as it should be, as it will help to set the feather with its curve correctly on the shaft. See Figure 60.

All the vanes on an arrow *must* be from feathers from the same side of the bird. A set of matched target arrows should also be all from one side of a bird.

If you have white feathers as well as gray, cut one white one to every two of the gray ones. This white feather will be the cock feather on the arrow, that is, the feathers that are fastened at right angles to the nock. See Figure 61. The other two are called hen feathers.

After the feathers are all ground down properly, take a thin shears, and, laying the feather down on the bench, hollow side up, cut off the surplus stem as shown in Figure 62.

Now a jig to hold the arrow while setting the

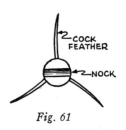

Fig. 61

Fig. 62

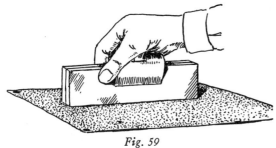

Fig. 59

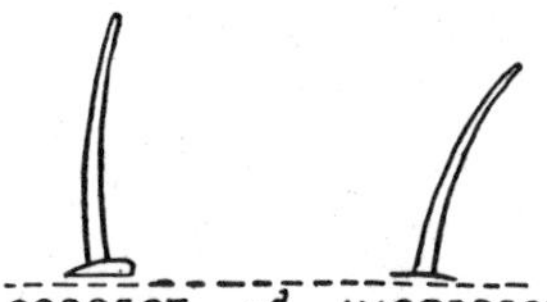

CORRECT *and* INCORRECT
GRINDING
Fig. 60

feathers in place is needed. In Figure 63 is shown one made of a box, the sides of which have been cut down to about 2 in. in height. In the center at one end, and ¼ in. from the upper edge, a hole 5/16 in. in diameter

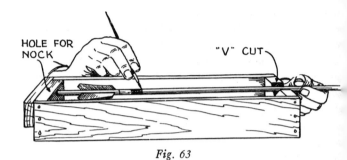

Fig. 63

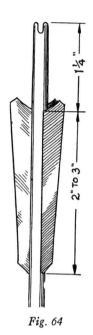

Fig. 64

has been bored. This is to take the nock end of the arrow, and a small piece of wood should be fastened over the outside of the box, so that the arrow, when placed in position, cannot slide through. At the other end, a V is cut. This should be deep enough so that the arrow lying in it will be parallel with the sides of the box. This box will also be used in painting crests.

The next step is to locate the positions of the vanes on the shaft. See Figures 61 and 64. Draw a line around the shaft 1¼ in. from the nock end and another 2 in. or so beyond that, depending upon how long the vanes are to be. Then run a line for the cock feather which should be located at right angles to the nock, using the fingers for a guide. The other two feathers should be located 1/3 of the circumference each side of

[32]

the cock feather. See Figure 65. With a little practice, it will be found easy to locate the positions of the three feathers. Next place the shaft in the box. If Dupont's household cement is to be used, run it along the stem of the vane, by holding the vane in the left hand and gently squeezing the cement out of the tube while moving it along. See Figure 66. One must work fast as this cement dries quickly, so as soon as the cement has been put on the vane, place the feather along the mark on the shaft. Be careful that the vane is perfectly straight and even, and press it down firmly on the shaft. If the right amount of cement is used, it will set in a short time. If too little is used, it will not hold well, while too much takes quite a while to set. The film of cement should be approximately 1/32 in. thick. Watch the vane for a few moments after letting go of it, to see that it is well fastened. Some fletchers use pins to hold the vanes in place until the glue has set properly. Then proceed to put on the other two. If possible, use a white feather for the cock feather. The other two should be natural dark feathers. If casein or fish glue is used, it is necessary to use pins to hold the feathers in place until the glue is dry.

Fig. 66

As the fletching on each arrow is finished, set it up on the drying board shown in Figure 67. This is made by boring 5/16-in. holes ¾ in. deep in a board 1 in. or more in thickness.

Next cut a brass or tin template to the shape chosen for the feathers. Lay this on the feather with the straight edge against the shaft, and trim off whatever

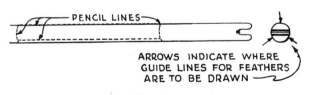

Fig. 65

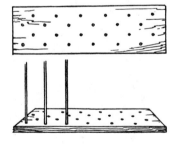

Fig. 67

extends beyond it, with a sharp shears. Figure 68 shows some of the shapes in use.

Trim off the forward end of each vane, where it is glued to the shaft, very carefully. Rough ends at these points may cut the archer's hand while shooting.

Target Arrows

Any arrow made out of a single piece of wood is called a self-arrow. Excellent self-arrows may be made of birch dowels. They can be purchased from dealers and manufacturers of millwork, cabinetwork, and upholsterers' supplies. They should be straight-grained and should be sanded very smooth. Straight-grained spruce, or pine, also makes good arrows. The best arrow shafts, however, are of Port Orford cedar which can be obtained at archery supply houses. If bought or cut in $3/8$-in. squares, they must be rounded. To do this, lay the square in the groove of the V board (see A, Figure 69), and plane off as shown. Then, turn it and do likewise with the other corners as shown at B, C, D, Figure 69. The shaft is now octagonal in shape. By laying it in the V with one edge up as at E, and taking off a little of each edge, a fairly round shaft is produced. Then sandpaper is used to take off the little corners that are left, leaving the shaft in the V and turning them continually while doing the sanding.

Shafts which are used for target work are tipped with parallel or bullet points (see Figure 70), the parallel being preferred, because they do not penetrate into the target so far. They cost about 3 cents each,

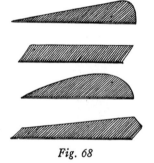
Fig. 68

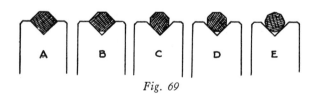
Fig. 69

and can be had in steel or brass. The shafts are whittled or filed down to a snug fit, as shown in Figure 71, after which the pile must be driven down carefully with a piece of wood. Be sure that the end of the shaft goes to the end of the pile and that the pile is on perfectly straight.

When Port Orford cedar, spruce, or pine shafts are used with a bow pulling 40 pounds or more, it is sometimes well to put a fiber spline into the nock end of the arrow to prevent splitting. For this purpose black or red fiber about 1/32 in. thick is used. With a fine saw, cut a slot about 1 in. long, this cut going in the same direction as the annual rings, as shown in Figure 72. Try out the saw cut first to see that the fiber fits in snugly. Then put fish glue or casein glue into the cut and on the spline and drive the latter in place. Wrap string around the end as shown in Figure 73A, or jam a clothespin over the end as shown in Figure 73B, and set aside. After the glue has dried thoroughly, cut away surplus fiber, and cut the nock at right angles to the fiber. The arrow is then ready to be finished. See Figure 74.

Before cutting the nock, examine each shaft to determine the direction in which the annual rings run. Then cut out the nock at right angles to these rings. See Figure 75.

The procedure to be followed for fletching target arrows is the same as that already described. Turkey pinion feathers are commonly used for target arrows, although goose feathers are preferable as they possess more oil than do turkey feathers, and therefore can

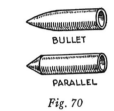

Fig. 70

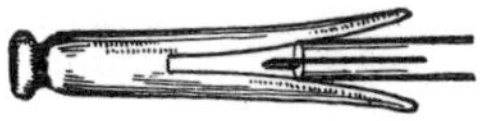

Fig. 71

Fig. 72

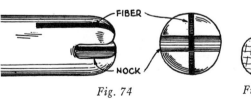

Fig. 74    *Fig. 75*

Fig. 73A

Fig. 73B

withstand dew and rain better. The wing feathers of hawks and large owls also make excellent arrow feathers, but are quite scarce.

After the glue on the vanes has dried thoroughly, the arrows are ready for the final finish. Most archers have their own private crest on each arrow. These are put on just forward of the feathers. They may be any combination of colors that appeals to the individual. The colors should be chosen carefully, because certain colors are easier to find in the grass than others.

There are several ways that may be used for finishing arrows:

a) The crest may be painted on the raw wood with water color, enamel, or colored lacquer, and the entire arrow then finished with white shellac.

b) The crest may be put on the raw wood with water colors and the entire arrow finished with clear lacquer.

c) The shaft may be shellacked first and the crest painted on with enamel or colored lacquer.

d) The shaft may be first lacquered with clear lacquer and a crest then painted on with colored lacquer.

No matter which method is chosen, no finish should be allowed to get into the nock.

Very fine black lines where two colors meet make the crest look more finished. See Figure 76. The archer who desires to have his name on his arrows may letter it between the vanes before the final coat of shellac or colorless lacquer is applied.

Fig. 76

Be sure to get this final coat over the glued parts on the vanes in order to prevent future damage due to moisture.

Hunting Arrows

Every man and boy interested in archery will at some time or other make some hunting arrows, regardless of the fact that very few ever get the chance to shoot anything larger than a rabbit. Hunting arrows, however, look very nice when made up. Indians used barrel-hoop-iron arrow heads, filed and fitted as shown in Figure 77. They usually tied these heads in place by wrapping wet sinews about the end of the shaft. The shrinking of the sinews as it dried, held the arrow head firmly.

The modern archer, however, is not satisfied with this type of hunting point. To make an up-to-the-minute hunting broad head, get some bronze 30-caliber bullet points, and some saw steel. Carefully saw a slot into the end of the bullet point, as shown at A, Figure 78, with a hack saw. Cut, file, or grind the saw steel to the shape shown at B in Figure 78, and drive it in place. Put the point on a piece of dowel rod for easy handling, and apply liquid flux. Then solder the two parts together. If the solder doesn't want to take hold as it should, put on more flux while the point is hot and try again. File off the surplus solder and file or grind a sharp but rough edge on the point.

These arrows are very dangerous and should be used with utmost care.

Fig. 77

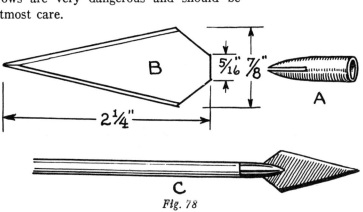

Fig. 78

Flight Arrows

Of all the types of arrows used today, the flight arrow is the lightest, thinnest, and most graceful. They should be made of light but tough wood. Port Orford cedar, Norway pine, and spruce are well suited for this purpose. They should be of the same length as the target arrows. At the tip and the nock they should be about 3/16 in. in diameter, and about 11 in. from the nock end it should be 5/16 in. or ¼ in. See Figure 79. This is what is called a barreled arrow and the taper from the thickest part to the ends should be graceful and gradual. Twenty-five caliber bullet-point tips are just right for flight arrows but they are hard to get. One of the writers made some aluminum and brass tips on a wood-turning lathe and has seen some made of horn and fiber. The arrow, however, should have some sort of tip to protect it in its fall.

The feathers should be thin and stiff. Turkey tail feathers make fine flight-arrow vanes. Make the vanes quite small — 1¼ to 1½ in. long, and 5/16 in. high seems to be a good size. See Figure 76.

The nock must be reinforced in some way. Thin tubular fiber ¼ in. outside diameter and ⅜ in. long may be fitted onto the shaft and glued on after which the nock is cut in. The nocks also may be reinforced by winding with silk set in glue.

Footed Arrows

Target arrows of Port Orford cedar, spruce, or pine are usually footed with hardwood. Beef wood and

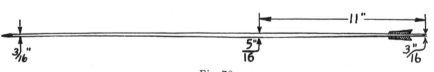

Fig. 79

lemonwood are the woods usually used, but walnut, maple, or hickory also are serviceable.

Footings are cut ⅜ in. square and 8 in. long, with a slot cut down the center about 5½ in. long, as shown in Figure 81. This slot should be cut parallel, *not at right angles,* to the annual rings.

Next take a 5/16-in. shaft and with a small sharp plane cut a 5¼-in. wedge shaped as shown in Figure 82, the thickness of the end to be the same as the width of the saw cut in the footing. Place the footing in the vise up to the saw cut (see Figure 83), put fish glue on the shaft and in the slot and force the shaft gently into the slot to the very bottom. Make sure that the footing is on straight and then wrap tightly with good stout cord. Set aside to dry for about 24 hours. Then unwind the cord and lay the shaft on a flat surface and with a sharp plane cut off the surplus wood, making the footing the same thickness as the shaft. Then turn it and plane the other sides until 5/16-in. square shaft is produced. See Figure 84. Lay the shaft in the V board and plane it round as you would any other shaft, always cutting away from the footing, toward the other end of the arrow. Then sandpaper the shaft, put on the pile, and finish.

Fig. 83

Blunt Arrows

After shooting with bows and arrows for a short time, the archer no doubt will marvel at the way an arrow can lose itself in even the shortest grass and how a pointed arrow can bury itself for an inch or so in a

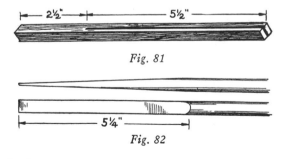

Fig. 81

Fig. 82

Fig. 84

tree trunk or branch so that it takes a half hour or more to dig it out.

For this kind of shooting, blunt arrows cannot be beat. If a lathe is available they may be turned easily but they also may be whittled out. Take a piece of maple or hickory ¾ in. square or round, and bore a 5/16-in. hole about ¾ in. deep in the end as straight as possible. See A, Figure 85. Put an arrow shaft in the hole to see how true it is. Whittle the head, 1⅝ in. long, to the shape shown at B. Put the shaft into the hole from time to time to be sure to get the head true. Next smooth it off nicely with a file or with coarse sandpaper. Then whittle it off as shown at C, after which it is glued onto the shaft. After the glue is thoroughly dry, sand off the end smoothly, and then give the entire arrow a coat of orange or red lacquer. These blunt arrows* have tremendous hitting power. They do not sneak under the grass as easily as do other arrows, but the chances of getting a rabbit with a blunt arrow are much better than with a hunting point. These blunt arrows will stand a lot of hard knocks too.

Remember to give all arrows a coating of shellac, lacquer, or varnish, and keep them in a reasonably dry place.

Rubbing an oiled rag over the arrows after shooting is well worth the effort and time it takes, and a little oil on the feathers does no harm either.

---

* Blunt arrow points may be bought under the name "Tear drop" points from L. C. Whiffen Co., Inc., 612 E. Clybourn St., Milwaukee, Wis., and as "Blunts" from the Warrior Archery Mfg. Co., 1821 So. First St., Milwaukee, Wis.

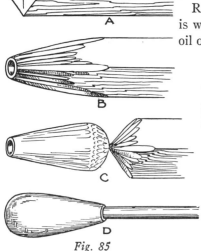

Fig. 85

Tackle

The Bracer

Now that the archer has a bow, a string, and some arrows, he may feel that he is ready to try them out. Before doing this, however, he will need a few more things. The most essential of these is the bracer or arm guard. The slap of a bowstring on the forearm is painful, to say the least. The skin is frequently broken, and a nasty bruise results. Coat or sweater sleeves will break the blow, but they also deflect the arrow. To avoid injury, therefore, one should have a bracer, such as is shown in Figure 87, made of stiff, smooth leather, or of a thin piece of wood. For the leather bracer, buy a piece of heavy calfskin at a harness or shoe shop.

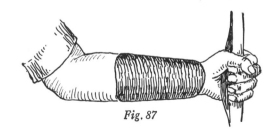

Fig. 87

Fig. 89

This must then be cut to shape as shown in Figure 88, and equipped with straps and buckles, or laces. If zippers such as are obtainable at the 5- and 10-cent stores are used, the leather should first be fitted to the arm. See Figures 89 and 90.

The wood arm guard, Figures 91 and 92, should be rounded to fit the forearm. The edges also should be rounded. The wood should be about ⅛-in. thick, 1½ to 2 in. wide, and 6 or 7 in. long. These arm guards are equipped with straps fastened with rivets or with glue into grooves cut for them. See Figure 92. After sanding, wood bracers should be decorated with water colors, after which several coats of spar varnish should be applied, rubbing down each coat with steel wool.

Finger Stalls

If the archer has tough fingertips, he can shoot in comfort. As a rule, however, a covering for the tips of the three shooting fingers is quite necessary when doing a lot of shooting, or when using a heavy bow. Dr. Elmer, in his book *Archery*, and Dr. Pope, in his *Hunting with Bow and Arrow*, both show what they consider proper finger stalls. Their suggestions are shown in Figures 93 and 94.

Fig. 90

These stalls should be made of calfskin or horsehide, or, lacking that, take leather from an old shoe.

Another method of protecting the fingertips is to put strips of ½-in. medicated tape along the fingers as shown in Figure 95. Gloves are used by many archers, some using a regular archer's glove while others take

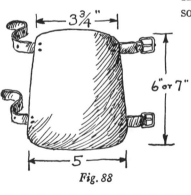

Fig. 88

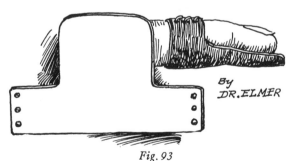

Fig. 93

[42]

an old glove and cut away the unnecessary portions. To prevent excessive wear, reinforce the tips of the fingers in these gloves with leather. Figure 96 shows sewn fingertips fastened to a wrist band with elastic bands.

The Quiver

A quiver is also very essential and there are many ways in which it may be made. The Indians made them of rawhide or buckskin, and sometimes used an entire

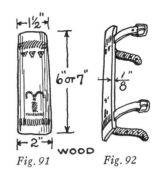

Fig. 91   Fig. 92

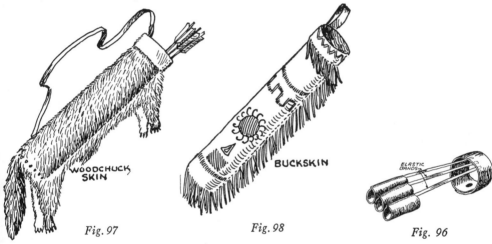

Fig. 97   Fig. 98   Fig. 96

fox, coon, or woodchuck skin with the fur, feet, and tail all left on. Figure 97 shows such a quiver. When making a quiver of leather or skin, or of any material

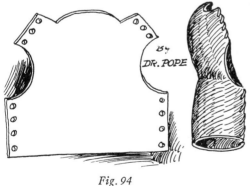

Fig. 94   Fig. 95

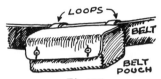

Fig. 102

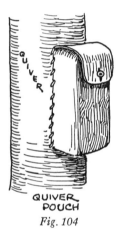

Fig. 104

Fig. 103

for that matter, it is well to make the bottom of some soft wood to prevent pointed arrows from piercing the material. If leather is not at hand, use canvas. Paint it several coats and then ornament it with colored paints.

Paper mailing tubes make serviceable quivers. Get one of the lighter kind, anywhere from 2 to 4 in. in diameter, and after fitting a piece of wood into the bottom, fasten it with a row of nails tacked all the way around. See Figure 99. The length of the quiver should be such that about 1 in. of the arrow shaft shows below the feathers. The feathers should never touch the quiver.

Quivers made of a mailing tube should be given a few coats of shellac inside and outside. To shellac the inside, pour some into the open end of the quiver. Then revolve and tip it gradually, until the entire inner surface is covered. After the shellac is dry, cover the outside with dark oilcloth, auto-top material, or leatherette. This is fastened into place with glue. Attach loops to the quiver as shown in Figures 98, 99, and 100, and suspend it from a belt. It is best to use a separate belt and not hang it on the one used to hold up the trousers. The quiver should hang from the right hip, somewhat toward the rear. The separate belt is advisable because in going through the wood and brush, the position of the quiver must be changed frequently. An archer who is left-handed, of course, will carry his quiver on the left side. For target work where only six arrows are used, a small flat quiver made of leather or a small

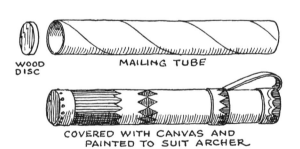

Fig. 99

mailing tube is all that is necessary. Such a quiver is shown in Figure 100.

The archer who wants to carry his bow along on auto tours or camping trips, will want a bow case to protect the bow while it is in transit. A nick in the back of a bow may mean a broken bow. Bow cases usually are made of canvas or of duck. They should be waterproofed and made a little longer than the bows for which they are intended so that the end may be lapped over and tied, or pulled up with a drawstring. See Figure 101.

The archer should also have a place to carry a few extras, such as an extra bowstring, some wax, an oiled rag, extra tips, etc. These may be carried in a leather case fastened to the belt as shown in Figure 102, or to the quiver, as shown in Figure 104, or the buckskin pouch shown in Figure 103 may be suspended from the quiver belt.

The Target

Having finished all his equipment, the archer will want something to shoot at. Regular straw targets may be purchased from dealers in archery equipment. They are made of rye or wheat straws about 4 in. thick and 4 ft. in diameter. They can be made at home if one has the necessary rye or wheat straw, marsh hay, or dried bullrushes. Such a straw target is made in much the same manner as that followed in making a grass table mat. The coils are made 4 in. thick, and they must be

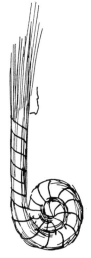

Fig. 105

Fig. 100

Fig. 101. Bow case

wrapped as tightly as possible with heavy cord. See Figure 105.

Keep adding material as you go along to keep the coil uniform, and until the length is sufficient to make the 4-ft. circle. This may mean 40 or more feet of 4-in. coil. Then roll it into a tight spiral, using a heavy upholsterer's needle to sew the adjacent coils together as the spiral is formed. Then cover the whole target with burlap sewed around the edge. The face of the target shown in Figure 106 is painted on sized muslin or sign painter's cloth. Do not use enamels or gloss paints.

The gold counts 9, the red, 7, the blue, 5, the black, 3, and the white, 1.

Fig. 107

Another target which is rather easy to make, but which is not portable, is made of two bales of straw set at an angle as shown in Figure 107.

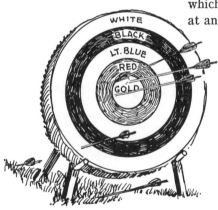

Fig. 106

The frame for this type of target may be made of 2 by 4-in. lumber or of 3-in. tamarack poles. The target face is then fastened to the straw with wood skewers. As this sort of target is out in all weather, it is well to provide a cover of some sort to keep off rain and snow, otherwise it will rot in a year or so.

Another form of target may be made of a 4-in. by 3 by 4-ft. carton of corrugated paper filled with straw or hay. Cartons of this kind may be obtained from printing establishments, as certain paper comes packed in them. A smaller target face will be necessary but it will be quite large enough to practice on.

Four or five thicknesses of corrugated strawboard, sewed together with heavy cord around the outer edge, also make a good target. These corrugated-paper targets may be made to regulation sizes, or they may be cut to resemble animal silhouettes for novelty shoots.

Target-Face Dimensions

Radii for drawing the circles

	3-Ft. Target	4-Ft. Target
Gold	3.6 in.	4.8 in.
Red	7.2 in.	9.6 in.
Blue	10.8 in.	14.4 in.
Black	14.4 in.	19.2 in.
White	18.0 in.	24.0 in.

Fig. 110

Fig. 113

Shooting

To be a good shot with the bow and arrow requires considerable practice. One of the first things the archer must acquire is the knack of stringing or bracing the bow. Figure 110 shows how this is done. Set the lower nock against the arch on the inside of the right foot (for left handers, the opposite holds). Then grasp the bow at the *grip* with the right hand and place the heel of the left hand on the back of the bow, near the top, with the fingers touching the loop. Press down with the left hand and at the same time pull with the right hand until the first two fingers of the left hand are able to slide the loop into the nock. In bracing the recurved bow, be careful to keep the thumb from getting under the string. The method shown and described is the one

Line-up at Milwaukee County Tournament

[48]

commonly used. It puts an equal strain on each limb of the bow, and is considered the best method for bracing a bow. With a little practice, it becomes quite simple.

In shooting, stand with the body at right angles to the target and with the head turned toward the target. For position, see Figure 111. The bow is held horizontally as shown in Figure 112, or sloping down somewhat as shown at A in Figure 113, the arrow being nocked with the cock feather up. The arrow in this position is at right angles to the string. Hold it with the first finger of the left hand and then extend the bow arm, turning the bow at the same time, from the horizontal to a vertical position. During all of this time, the three fingers of the right hand are holding the arrow in position on the string while the first finger of the left hand is holding it in place against the bow as shown in Figure 112. Now take the finger off the arrow at the bow, allowing the latter to lie free in the angle of the hand and the bow, as illustrated in Figure 114. Keep the left arm straight (see B, Figure 113) and pull back the string with the fingers of the right hand until it is about at the middle of the cheek. See C, Figure 113. When ready to release the arrow, slowly straighten out the tips of the fingers of the right hand, allowing the string to roll over the fingertips. See D, Figure 113. This may seem difficult to those accustomed to using the pinch grip on small weak bows, but a beautiful release is made by this method. There are other releases, but compared to them, the one described is

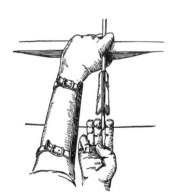

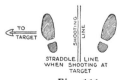

Fig. 111

Fig. 112
Note: *Hold arrow as shown only while getting ready to shoot. Before shooting remove upper finger from arrow and allow the latter to lie free in the angle formed by the hand and bow, or on the arrow rest if there is one.*

Maj. Chas. L. Williams, testing junior tackle built for little archers

quite simple. *Do not* try to shoot while the finger of the left hand is over the arrow. The left-hand finger grip shown in Figure 112 is used only while waiting to shoot or while walking along when hunting. As shown in Figure 112, the string is pulled back just a little bit, thus producing enough tension on the string so that it is easy to keep the arrow in place with the forefinger while walking through the fields or woods. As soon, however, as the archer starts to draw, the forefinger grip is relaxed and the bow is gripped as shown in Figure 114.

Roving

Few archers, whether boys or men, own a target at the beginning. While waiting to acquire a target, considerable practice may be gained by indulging in roving shoots. Equipped with bow, bracer, finger guards, and a quiver full of arrows, get out in the country where there is plenty of room. A closely cropped pasture is ideal for roving, provided the cows or sheep are no longer in the pasture, or at least are out of bow shot. Every weed or small bush may be looked upon as a target. Even the tall mullein stalks make excellent wands to shoot at. It adds interest to roving if the smaller weeds are looked upon as representing rabbits, while the larger bushes may represent deer and bears. The archer should remember that the bow should be pulled to the cheek for every shot.

A real roving course may be laid out, and definite rules set up for it. Rabbits, squirrels, woodchucks,

Fig. 114

partridges, pheasants, and the like, may be cut from some material like beaverboard or celotex, and before the shoot, someone may be commissioned to locate these at different places over the pasture. The cut-outs may be anywhere from 20 to 50 yds. or more apart. When the first one is sighted, each archer takes as many shots as have been decided upon, after which the scores are marked. When the next cut-out is sighted, each one shoots at this, and so on. The course may be laid out so that the game can be sighted only from certain points and so that only one cut-out can be seen at a time. A lot of fun and good archery practice may be had on a course of this kind.

Wand Shooting

Wand shooting is simply shooting at a straight stick of soft wood 1 or 2 in. wide and 6 ft. high. These sticks are pointed at one end so they may be driven into the ground. The strength of the bow should determine the distance at which the archer is to shoot.

200-lb. wild boar killed at 50 yds., with one arrow, by Howard Hill

Target Shooting

Just as it is considered bad form in golfing if a bystander does anything to distract a golfer about to make a drive, so it is bad form to distract an archer about to shoot at an archery meet. Archery, therefore, is an orderly and peaceful pastime offering plenty of exercise, shooting, walking, and stooping.

An end in archery means six arrows. After each contestant shoots an end, or six arrows, whether the arrows

are shot in two's, three's, or all six, one after another, the archers lay or hang their bows away and all walk to the target together. Then, while one man pulls all the arrows belonging to one archer from the target, he calls the score, so that the score keeper can mark it down. The puller then takes the next person's arrows and calls them, and so on, until all contestants have been scored. Meanwhile there are always a few arrows that did not hit the target. These must be found. Everyone helps look for lost arrows in order that the game is held up as little as possible. Then all walk back and begin shooting another end. No one should under any conditions shoot until every archer is on the line. The rules for tournaments and shoots are as given here.

Tournaments

Rules for different tournaments vary. In archery, the term "round" signifies the number of arrows shot at a 4-ft. target at a given distance, and are classified as follows:

York Round — 72 arrows at 100 yds., 48 arrows at 80 yds., 24 arrows at 60 yds., a total of 144 arrows.

Metropolitan Round — 30 arrows at 100 yds., 30 arrows at 80 yds., 30 arrows at 60 yds., 30 arrows at 50 yds., 30 arrows at 40 yds., a total of 150 arrows.

American Round — 30 arrows at 60 yds., 30 arrows at 50 yds., 30 arrows at 40 yds., a total of 90 arrows.

Columbia Round — 24 arrows at 50 yds., 24 arrows at 40 yds., 24 arrows at 30 yds., a total of 72 arrows.

Junior American Round — 30 arrows at 50 yds., 30

Pat Chambers, National Champion, 1938, San Francisco

Standing left to right: Gene Warnick (men's flight, 462 yds.), Curtis Hill (men's free style, 610 yds.), Merta Longley (junior girls' double Columbian and double American, total 2,255), Sonny Johns (junior boys, total 2,710).
Front row, Pat Chambers (3,012, high national total for all time), Jean Tenney (2,027, high national total).

arrows at 40 yds., 30 arrows at 30 yds., a total of 90 arrows.

Junior Columbia Round — 24 arrows at 40 yds., 24 arrows at 30 yds., 24 arrows at 20 yds., a total of 72 arrows.

Archery Golf

This is a very pleasant game which can be played with no casualties to the stock of arrows. To play it, one should have a couple of flight arrows, a putting arrow and a cloth ball about 5 in. in diameter filled with straw or excelsior. The putting arrow should be a birch arrow with a pointed nail in the end, which prevents the arrow from skipping or snaking in the green. The game is played over a regular golf course, the flight arrow being used for the drives and the putting arrow is naturally used for putting. Take a good golfer along as an opponent. When near the green or cup, place the cloth ball about a foot or two over to one side of the cup and shoot at it. The golfer will putt for the cup. If the arrow hits less than a bow length from the ball, there is no need to shoot again — just call it a stroke or shot.

It is always best to ask the attendant of the golf course for permission to use the bow and arrows, and it is well to play when no one is playing in front of the archers.

*Ken Kilhelm,
Los Angeles, Hunter,
Archer, extraordinary*

Flight Shooting

Flight shooting is one of the events of a tournament. Each archer usually having a bow especially built for this purpose. The contestants shoot from three to six arrows each. The archers in this event are separated into 3 classes — men, women, and juniors. The measuring is done with a tapeline.

Bruce Robertson shooting free style. — Photograph, courtesy of The Milwaukee Journal

Modern Dianas. — Photograph, courtesy of The Milwaukee Journal

One of the requirements for a merit badge for archery in scout work, is to shoot an arrow a prescribed distance. For this purpose, flight arrows are used. To get the most distance out of an arrow, the elevation should be about 45 deg. As a flight arrow is a rather delicate affair, choose a level field, preferably a golf course where the ground is not too hard or stony. Be careful *not* to overdraw the bow; it may not be able to take it.

Clout Shooting

This contest usually follows the target shooting in tournaments. A center for the target is made of white paper 4 ft. in diameter. This is laid upon the ground, and circles are made around it with powdered lime or flour to make a target anywhere from 24 ft. to 48 ft. in diameter.

The white center is used because it can be seen easily. A few arrows are shot by each contestant to get the proper elevation after which each one shoots 5 ends or 30 arrows. The distance from the center may be from 100 yds. to 180 yds., depending upon the bows used. It is usually taken as 180 yds. for men, 130 yds. for women, and 100 yds. for juniors. The count is the same as on a regulation target.

Animal target

Novelty Shoot

To provide a diversion from regular target shooting, lifesize (or nearly so) animal silhouettes may be pasted or painted on a thickness of four or five sheets of corrugated strawboard which are sewed together with strong cord on the outside edges.

Set these targets out on the range at varying distances, so that the archers must judge the distances themselves. The animals should be marked with thin lines so that the vulnerable spots count highest, a mere scratch or wound counting only one point. The captain places a piece of cord or tape on the ground at random. This then serves as the line from which the archers are to shoot, and none of them will know the exact distance to the target.

To add still more interest to these novelty shoots, the animal targets may be made to run along a rope trolley by suspending the target from two ropes fastened to small pulleys. The targets may then be pulled back and forth along the trolley.

Animal target

Hunting

We now come to the part of archery which every man and boy is anxious to try. Wonderful wild-game shooting has been done by men like Arthur Young,

A buffalo which fell victim to Howard Hill's arrow

Milwaukee archers and their animal target

Jeanne Hunt trying for a red squirrel

Saxton Pope, Steward Edward White, Howard Hill, and others. Every kind of game in North America has been brought down with arrows, while lions, tigers, panthers, etc., have been bagged in Africa.

Such hunting, however, is reserved for the very few. Almost every year, there are a few men enthusiasts who go deer hunting with bows and arrows and several deer are brought down each season. The boys, however, can have a lot of fun during the hunting season, shooting rabbits, squirrels, pheasant, partridge, quail, plover, snipe, and even wild ducks. With ducks, unless one is a pretty good shot, a miss usually means a lost arrow.

Our advice to boys and even men, when shooting small game, is to use blunt arrows. A rabbit will run away with an ordinary target or hunting arrow through him, and while you may eventually get him, chances of getting him are better if he has been hit with a blunt arrow. Then, too, if the archer misses, the chances of finding the arrow are better if the blunt arrows are used. The same holds true when hunting squirrels, as there will be no need to climb trees and dig out pointed arrows.

Naturally, blunt arrows do not fly so far as do the ordinary arrows, but in hunting with the bow and arrow, one must do as the Indians did, stalk the game quietly or lie in wait for it.

Blunt arrows also are safer. One of the writers, as a boy, was playing "Indian" with his companions. They were armed with bows and blunt arrows. One of the boys, shooting over a pile of brush, hit the writer's younger brother squarely on the chin. What would have happened had that arrow been anything but a blunt one? With all archery practice and sport, it must always be kept in mind that the bow and arrow is a very dangerous weapon, and that it should be handled with the greatest of care.

Be sure no one is within range and don't ever shoot over or through brush or trees which might hide persons or animals. An arrow flying through the air has much force behind it, and it must at all times be looked upon as a very dangerous missile.

Care of Archery Tackle

Now, just a few words about the care of archery tackle.

After shooting, unstring the bow and wipe it and the arrows with an oiled rag or with wax. This forms a protecting film over the wood and varnish, and adds to the life of the bow and the arrows. Wax the string.

Store the bow and arrows in a moderately dry, cool place when not in use.

Hang up the bow. This will tend to keep it from bending out of shape.

The arrows should be laid away where nothing will be placed on them, otherwise they may become distorted and rendered useless.

Do not let inexperienced people string and pull your bow. A bow over which you have labored long and strenuously is easily ruined.

Check the string from time to time. If the whipping at eye or center shows signs of fraying, replace it.

The archer will be amply repaid by the better performance of his archery tackle if he gives it just a bit of extra care.

Howard Hill stalking

Short Cuts

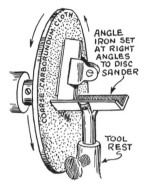

Fig. 115

The foregoing chapters show how archery tackle may be made with a minimum of tools. In this home-shop era, however, there are many ways in which this type of work may be simplified. The band saw, the jointer, the lathe and sanding disk, and electricity are a great help. The jointer may be used to straighten out the back of the bow and to dress down the gluing surface of the grip.

The band saw comes in handy in cutting out the bow and also when making footings.

The lathe is used for sanding arrows, and for turning blunt points for arrows. The disk sander may be used for grinding feathers. Figure 115 shows how this is done. Figure 116 shows an end mill chucked in the lathe for cutting down the end of the arrow to fit the pile. The end mill shown in Figure 117 is made out of a piece of $\frac{1}{8}$-in. pipe. With a twist drill, bore out the inside of this pipe to the correct diameter. No exact dimensions can be given for this because all piles or points are not the same size. Then file the teeth as shown, and drive a plug in from the end opposite the teeth. This plug acts as a stop and its position must be determined by the pile that is to be used on the arrows. Before starting the shaft in the end mill, bevel off the shaft end slightly with a pencil sharpener. The kind that can be bought for a dime will answer nicely. Figure 116 shows a steady rest which may be used for keeping

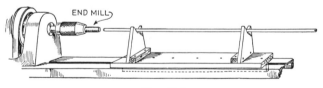

Fig. 116

Fig. 117

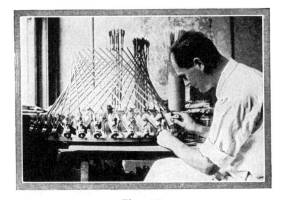

Fig. 118

the arrow shaft in proper alignment while using the end mill.

After one gets more interested in shooting, the matter of arrows takes on added importance. When many arrows are to be fletched, the hand method is found to be too slow. There are several fletching jigs on the market, but a simple jig that is very efficient can easily be made. Figure 118 shows how Larry Whiffen, Milwaukee, Wisconsin, an expert archer, bowyer, and fletcher, fletches 48 arrows at one time. That is the pro-

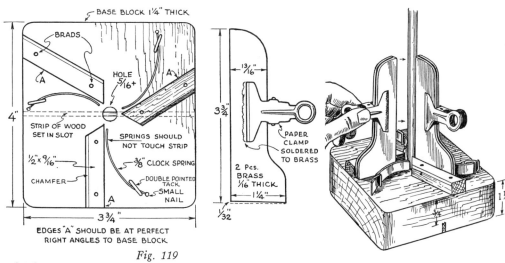

Fig. 119

fessional way. The jig shown in Figure 119 does the work very well. If several of these jigs are at hand, the cement or glue on the first arrows will set while the feathers are being glued to other arrows. The important part is that the three cleats and the hole are at right angles with the board. This will enable the springs to hold the feather clamps in alignment with the shaft. A small rubber band slipped over the three clamps will help to keep the pressure even. The clamp should be cut at a slight angle. This gives added accuracy in case the shaft does not set perfectly straight. File a notch at the lower edge of the clamp to show where the end of the feather should be. It should set the feathers $1\frac{1}{4}$ in. from the nock.

If a piece of cardboard is placed between the two pieces of brass when these are soldered to the clamps, the feathers will be held more firmly. The clock springs should not touch the cleats when the clamp has been removed, otherwise they may pinch the feathers and rip them off when the arrow is being removed. (To remove the clamps, simply press them open and pull them away from the shaft.)

If there are many arrows to be fletched, it may pay to make the feather-trimming jig shown in Figure 120. This jig is easily made and requires the purchase of but a few inexpensive electrical parts.

After the nichrome trimming wire has been shaped to the desired contour of the feather, place the fletched arrow into the jig with the nock end pressed firmly

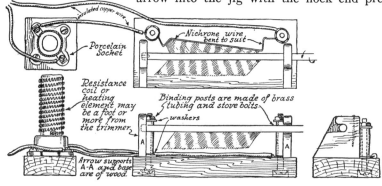

Fig. 120

against the left-hand support. By twirling the arrow, the hot wire will singe off the feathers, producing smooth, uniform vanes in a twinkling.

Some archers delight in using brightly colored cock feathers on their arrows. It is difficult, however, to find dyes that can be used successfully for coloring these feathers. However, if colored feathers are desired, they usually can be obtained from the regular archery supply dealers.

When sanding arrows on the lathe, it is best to put the piles on first. The pile may then be clamped into the chuck without danger of spoiling the shaft. If the shaft is perfectly true, the loose end may be steadied with the hand. A little experimenting will acquaint the archer with the action of an arrow shaft on the lathe. If the free end of the shaft whips about very much, a hollow dead center also may be used to steady the shaft.

The sandpaper book shown in Figure 121 may be anywhere from 6 to 12 in. long. When in use, it must be moved from end to end over the arrow, and never held in one place for any length of time. Coarse sandpaper is used for roughing, and fine sandpaper for finishing. The sandpaper, or better still, garnet cloth, should be glued into the grooves of the sandpaper book.

More and more archers are beginning to put arrow rests on their bows. The reasons for this are twofold. A feather will sometimes be a little rough or sharp at the end and will give the archer a nasty cut. This may,

Fig. 121

of course, be overcome by wrapping the forward part of the feather with fine silk and applying shellac over it. An arrow rest will obviate this trouble from the start. Figures 122 and 123 show how the arrow rest may be made and fastened to the bow. Another reason for the arrow rest is that it places the arrow at exactly the same place on the bow each time. To fix the placing of the arrow still more definitely on the bow, a piece of colored silk may be wrapped about the string at the nocking point. Some archers wrap the bowstring so as to produce a slight bulge above the nocking point. The arrow is then set snugly against this bulge, thus definitely nocking it at the same point for each shot.

Arrow rests may be made of a variety of wood, fiber, brass, horn, or aluminum. All edges on the rest should be rounded off smoothly so as not to damage the shaft or the feathers.

At tournaments or any target shooting, there are various ways of carrying the arrows. A careful examination of the illustration forming the chapter head on page 5 shows that each of the first four men has a different way of doing so. The third man from the left uses the wire arrow holder or ground quiver shown in Figure 124. When the archer is ready to walk to the target, the bow is hung by the string over the hook shown at A in Figure 124. It is a better method than laying the bow on the damp grass or on the ground where it may be stepped on. The first and fourth men shown in this illustration, carry their arrows in the hip

Fig. 122

Fig. 123

Fig. 124

and side pockets of their trousers. If this latter method is used, it is well to line the pockets with leather in order to protect them against wear.

A piece of equipment frequently noticed at tournaments is the arrow case. Almost every archer has one, and many of them display the skill, patience, and ingenuity expended upon them by their makers. In these cases are carried the arrows, spare strings, wax, extra tips, glue, cement, finger stalls, arm guard, etc. They also frequently contain the picturesque little hat with its feather which some archers wear and which adds color to the tournaments. These arrow cases have racks, each of which can hold 6 arrows, as shown in Figure 125. The space at the ends is used for holding the other items enumerated before. These boxes are usually made 8 in. square, from 30 to 36 in. long. Thin plywood is used for the sides, top, and bottom, the ends being of thicker wood.

Some of these cases are stained and varnished, some are painted and some are covered with leather or auto-top material. Metal corners are used on some of the cases, and the covers are closed with hasps or auto-trunk latches. They are equipped with a handle for carrying and some are protected with special locks. Many archers make arrow cases strong enough to serve as seats while watching others shoot.

Figure 126 is a wiper made of wool yarn which is seen frequently at tournaments and at archery golf. It hangs from the belt and is used to wipe mud or moisture from the arrows.

Fig. 125

Fig. 126

Emergency Arrows

There are times when the things needed for making arrows are not at hand. One can readily make them, however, by using whatever shafts are available, such as dried willow or ash shoots, or doweling; and for fletching, the tail feathers of pigeons, chickens, ducks, or wild birds.

Figure 127 shows how these emergency arrows may be fletched. Two feathers, for each arrow, are trimmed, as shown at *a*, Figure 127, with shears or knife. The ends of the feathers are then tied to the nock end as shown at *b*. The feathers are then carefully bent over and wrapped as shown at *c*.

To finish off such emergency arrows, char the points of the shafts, or wrap them with wire. Such arrows, while inexpensive, will be found to be serviceable and to fly very nicely.

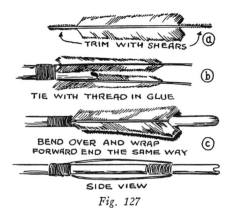

Fig. 127

Flat Bows from Square Staves

Square bow staves of lemonwood, hickory, yew, Osage orange, or locust also may be utilized for making flat bows. While these square staves are more expensive than the flat, they do away with the necessity of gluing on a handle or grip. Square bow staves of yew, Osage orange, and locust are split out of the log and trimmed roughly into staves 2 to 2½ in. square and 6 ft. long, as shown in Figure 128. In making a bow out of such a stave, the back or bark side should be leveled off first, the natural grain of the wood being followed lengthwise. Small bumps are usually leveled off. Figure 129 shows how the back should be made with a slight curve to follow the annual rings of the wood. The stave is then cut into a 1⅛ to 1¼-in. square, always following the grain as much as possible.

After finishing this part of the work, the lengthwise profile of the bow may look like any one of the staves shown in Figure 128. In making a bow of yew, the white wood or sapwood which lies immediately under the bark is carefully trimmed down to about 3/16 in. This acts as a natural backing which helps to keep the bow from breaking.

Lemonwood and hickory staves are usually sawed into 1 or 1⅛-in. squares, and are, therefore, quite a bit easier to make into bows. Sight along the stave to see how straight it is. If it is bent like Figure 130, take the hollow side for the back of the bow. This will give the same effect as setting back the bow, of which more will be said later on.

Fig. 128

Fig. 130

Fig. 129

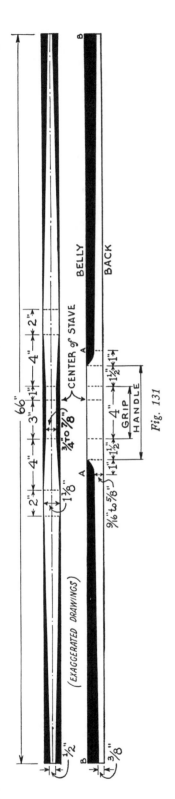

Fig. 131

Making the Bow

Cut the stave to a length of from 5 ft. 6 in. to 5 ft. 10 in. Next, locate the center of the stave, and, using a try-square, draw lines across the belly and the sides. See Figure 131. Then lay off the *grip,* by locating points 3 in. on one side, and 1 in. on the other, measuring from the *center of the stave.* Draw lines through these points, squaring them across belly, sides, and back.

Then following the layout as shown in the side view in Figure 131, draw lines at a distance of 1½ in. each side of the grip. The 7-in. space thus laid out, forms the *handle.* Draw two more lines 1 in. beyond each end of the handle. Measuring from the back, lay off the thickness of the bow 9/16 to ⅝ in. on the lines last drawn. The thickness at the ends of the bow is made ⅜ in. as shown. Finally draw lines from A to B (see Fig. 131), and connect the ends of the handle and the points at AA with a graceful curve. If the stave is bent as shown in Figure 130, straighten it out by clamping it to a straight surface while making the layout just described.

Cut out the side profile of the bow either by hand or with a band saw.

Next, turn the bow with its back upward, and draw a center line along its full length. A stave that is badly warped, for instance, one like that shown in Figure 132, which has no side that is perfectly flat, cannot be made into a good bow. Slightly warped staves, however, can be used by laying off the center line as

Fig. 132

directed in Figure 2, page 6, so as to get the most out of the stave.

Lay off the grip, which should be ¾ to ⅞ in. wide, so that the center line of the stave passes through its center. Then lay off lines 4 in. from each end of the grip, and again 2 in. beyond these marks, as shown in the top view of Figure 131. The width of the bow in these 2-in. spaces is made 1⅛ in., and the ends of the bow are made ½ in. wide. Connect all the points established, with lines, as shown, and cut away the surplus wood. The final shaping of the bow is done by following the directions given on page 8.

The grip is rounded as shown in Figure 133. If desired, the grip may be covered with leather or wrapped with cord as described on page 10.

Fig. 133

Setting Back a Bow

Setting back a bow at the grip gives the bow a better cast and a better shape. Figure 134, shows how a set-back bow looks when unstrung, and also when strung or braced.

To form this set-back, square up the stave and then make the usual layout upon it, using good strong pencil lines. Then put a pailful of water into a wash boiler, lay the bow across the top so that the middle of the bow is in the middle of the boiler, place the wash-boiler cover over the bow, and then pile a few old rugs or burlap bags over all to conserve the steam. Let the water boil for at least one hour.

While the bow is steaming, get the bending jig ready. There are several ways in which the bending

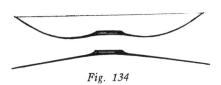

Fig. 134

may be done. The easiest one is to use a vise and heavy bar of iron about 1½ in. square and from 16 to 18 in. long, as shown in Figure 135. Place a block of wood in the vise thick enough to hold the iron level with the jaws (see Fig. 136). Then cut two blocks of pine 2 by 2 by 2 in. and round off one side as shown in Figure 135. Bore a hole in each of the blocks and wire them to the ends of the iron bar as shown. If no iron bar is available a piece of oak or maple about 3 or 4 in. square will do the trick. The bar is set on the block and the vise opened so the bow stave will fit between the end blocks and the rear vise jaws.

After the stave has been steamed an hour or more, remove it and as quickly as possible, place it in the vise, putting a block of soft wood between it and the jaw, and then slowly tighten up until the stave has a set-back of about 3 to 3½ in. The set-back may be measured with a straight edge as shown in Figure 137.

Watch carefully when the bending is going on, and at the first sign of cracking or splitting, loosen up the vise a bit. Sometimes a little cross grain, or not enough steaming, will cause the stave to splinter. Rather than break an otherwise good stave, it would

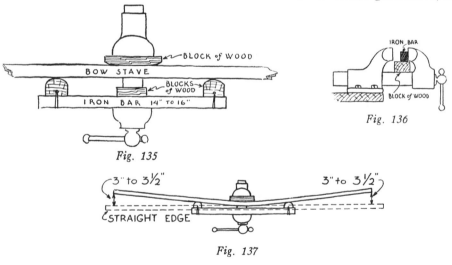

Fig. 135

Fig. 136

Fig. 137

be best just to make a straight bow, or one with not so much set-back.

Another way that a stave may be bent is to use two "C" clamps as shown in Figure 138. Do the bending by tightening the clamps alternately, until the stave is bent sufficiently.

Allow the stave to stay in the clamps or vise for 12 hours or more before removing it and then do not try to bend it for at least two weeks. The bow may be roughed out but it should not be tillered until the two weeks have elapsed.

The roughing out and finishing is, of course, done as with any other bow. The set-back bow will be well worth the extra work put upon it.

In bracing a set-back bow, the string should be the usual fistmele from the grip.

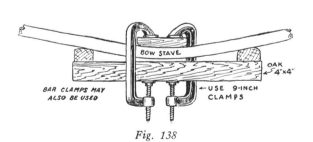

Fig. 138

The end — of the bunny

Index

Animal targets, 55
Archery golf, 53
Arm guard, 41
Arrow case, 63
Arrow drying board, 33
Arrowheads, Indian, 37
Arrow rests, 61, 62
Arrow wiper, 63
Arrows, 27
Arrows, blunt, 39, 40, 56
Arrows, emergency, 64
Arrows, finishing, 36
Arrows, flight, 38
Arrows, footed, 38
Arrows, hunting, 37
Arrows, inexpensive, 28
Arrows, sanding, 34, 61
Arrows, target, 34

Band saw, 58
Belt pouch, 44
Bending form, 13
Blunt arrows, 39, 40, 56
Bow, care of, 20, 57
Bow case, 45
Bow, made from square staves, 65
Bow, recurved, 11
Bow, set-back, 67
Bow staves, 6, 65
Bow, weight of, 9
Bow woods, 6
Bows, backed, 15
Bowstring, 22
Bracer, leather, 41
Bracer, wood, 42
Bracing, 11, 48
Broad heads, 37
Bullet points, 35

Care of bow, 20, 57
Care of tackle, 57
Case, arrow, 63
Casein glue, 16
Checks, 15
Clout shooting, 54
Colored feathers, 61
Crests, 36

Decorating box, 32
Drying board, arrow, 33
Directions for shooting, 48

Emergency arrows, 64
End, 51
End mill, 88

Feather cement, 33
Feather clamp, 30, 59, 60
Feather dye, 61
Feather grinding, 31, 58
Feather template, 33
Feather trimmer, 60
Fiber-backed bow, 17
Finger stalls, 42
Finishing arrows, 36
Finishing bows, 19
Fistmele, 11
Fletching, 29
Fletching box, 32
Fletching jig, 59
Flight arrows, 38
Flight shooting, 53
Flight shooting records, 54
Footed arrows, 38

Glue, 16
Gluing, 16
Grinding feathers, 31, 57
Grip or handle, 10
Gripping the bow, 49, 50
Ground quiver, 62

Handle, 10
Hickory, 6, 65
Hickory-backed bow, 15
Hunting, 55
Hunting arrow, 37

Indian arrowheads, 37
Inexpensive arrows, 28

Lathe, 57
Lemonwood, 6, 65
Locust, 6, 65
Loop, 23

Nock, reinforced, 9, 35
Nocks, 8, 12, 13, 29
Nocks, molded, 29
Novelty shoot, 55

Oiling arrows, 40, 56
Oiling bows, 20, 56
Osage orange, 6, 65

Parallel points, 35
Planing jig, 28, 34
Planing shafts, 34
Points, bullet, 35
Points, parallel, 35
Port Orford cedar, 34
Pouches, 44
Pull of bow, 9

Quiver, 43, 44, 45, 62
Quiver pouch, 44

Rawhide-backed bow, 19
Recurved bow, 11
Reinforced nock, 9, 35
Release, 49
Rounds, 52
Roving, 50

Sanding arrows, 34, 61
Sanding disk, 58
Sandpaper book, 61
Serving string, 26
Set back bow, 67
Shooting, 48
Shooting position, 49
Short cuts, 57
Spacing feathers, 32
Steaming, 12

Tackle, 41
Target arrows, 34
Target etiquette, 51
Target shooting, 51
Targets, 45, 46, 47, 55
Tillering, 8
Tillering jig, 8
Tournaments, 52
Trimmer for feathers, 60
Trimming feathers, 33, 60

V board, 28, 34

Walnut bow, hickory backed, 15
Wand shooting, 51
Waxed string, 25
Weight of bow, 9
Wiper, arrow, 63

Yew, 6, 65

[70]